SPECTRUM

A Plethora of Rhapsody

An anthology of poetry

Laldinkima Sailo

Books For All
Delhi-110052

Distributed by
D. K. Publishers Distributors Pvt. Ltd.
24, Ansari Road,
New Delhi-110 002
Phs. : 327 8368, 326 1465, 320 1514
Fax : 326 4368
E-mail : dkpd@del3.vsnl.net.in
Web site:www.dkpd.com.

First Published : 2002

ISBN 81-7386-243-5

Published by
Books For All
(an imprint of Low Price Publications)
A-6, Nimri Commercial Centre,
Near Ashok Vihar Phase-IV,
Delhi-110 052
Ph. : 740 1672, 745 2453
E-mail : Ipp@nde.vsnl.net.in
Web site:www.Ippindia.com.

Printed at
D. K. Fine Art Press Pvt. Ltd.
Delhi-110052 Ph. 745 2451

Printed in India

To God and his greatest manifestations of inspiration for me in this Earth - My 'Great' grandfathers - the late Mr. Robula and Brig. T. Sailo

Foreword

The last time I met Laldinkima, he was on his way to joining the Bishop Cotton School at Shimla. I did not know that he wrote poetry, and could never have imagined that he would return a few years later with a collection of his poems. This collection of poems is many things at once. It is always reflective, talking the reader through a multitude of thoughts, emotions, and events. It is perceptive, sensing things that lie beyond the obvious. It is also imaginative, finding words that create living images. It is the thought and work of one between the age of 14 to 16 years.

Some of the poems are abstract reflections, on life and on relationships, sprinkled with a wisdom that is often tinged with sadness. *Unto Whence* talks of the futility of material desire, *Acceptance* of the virtue of labour and *Twist and Sham* of the crumbling institution of marriage. Other poems delve into the inexorability of time, on the power of imagination, loneliness, on beauty, and on friendship. *To eternity* traces the bond between siblings where 'The intimate closeness/ the loving care...' is lost with time. The poet comments on the 'magic of memory', 'the quality of which depends widely from how a time at hand is spent/ to how good a recollection is made' in *With a living past.*

Equally engrossing are the stories that the poet tells. Of how David humbled Goliath, 'The pebble that hit the giant/ Possessed a greater faith than the giant himself...' in *Courage in Faith.* Of a trouble land where 'At once a thousand pagodas/ beautifully scattered...' was shattered by the 'tyranny of a merciless brigand', to a place where 'The temple is now a sham/ a business place of evil' in *The sun may rise again.* In a poignant account of one excluded from celebrating the anniversary of a free nation, *14th August*...takes us 'Through the streets and paths of the city/ thundering sparks of 'nationalism'/ where I unnoticed lay on four'. *An Unsung Hero* makes his way 'In the wilderness of the jungle/ between the heat of beasts/ where life rises and falls/ upon the metre of death'. These and other narratives stand out for the tales they tell as well as for their beautiful choice of words. Love lost through 'distant words too softly spoken', the 'sweet pleasure of disobedience' in cutting classes at school, the childlike pleasure as 'dark warning clouds splat the sky' and 'the sweet delight of illiteracy' all conjure up feelings that are buried within us.

A third set of poems focus on specific characters. *In Conscientiousness* tells us of a man of deep conviction, 'Shielded in a hardness of a walnut/ Is his conscience...'. A seemingly more personal touch is seen in *My Friend: a Science Student*, who pursues his interest against all odds; *Buddy*, a friendship where 'We exchanged our shadows/ and so as we depart I bear/ his shadow and he mine'; and, *Humour of a Bookworm* to whom '...sinful is his idea of the cafeteria/ even worse is to merry make with friends.'

The Second Last Chapter of Volume I is about leaving school, of nostalgia, of parting and of a new beginning. I would add that this is also a time for new encounters, with people, places, and relationships. I do hope that in these, Laldinkima finds the inspiration and the commitment to further develop the creative talent that he obviously possesses.

Daman Singh

Preface

Spectrum: A Plethora of rhapsody is an endeavour to return what little I have to the world which has given me so much. It is also a view-point of a sixteen year old about the way he sees life and it's supplements. However, many and different age groups will also agree with me on my views and I am sure will find pleasure in reading this anthology. It includes a wide range of topics, from the likes of humour out of a friend to looking at ourselves from our darker and happier sides. Since the book is like a thought process of mine, I have not put the poems in any order of classification. It would indeed be very difficult to arrange one's thoughts since one does not know what he is about to think!

All the poems may not bear a 'rapturous' nature but all of them has evolved out of great inspiration, enthusiasm and come with a strong feeling. The persons to whom the book is dedicated to also bear important significance since many of the poems idolize their characters and ways of life.

Through the course of the book, I have often used the word 'conscience', in trying to bring forth an idea of believing in oneself and when I speak of 'conscience', I assume that it is always guided by God. Likewise, I have brought out this book believing in myself-my conscience under the guidance of God.

I hope the reader finds stimulation and delight in reading the book and I shall be open to discussions on any of the works included in this collection.

Laldinkima Sailo

Prologue:
A Prayer of Retrospection and Optimism.

Many a sins I committed,
Well written are the horrid deeds
in sparkling letters upon mine epitaph.
Since long I had been dead,
Submerged in the sinful pool of death.
As for the living body of a dead soul
Whose strength merele comes from his bread
most befit a sulking owl.

Cling I to the hopes of my undone deeds
that what little I may do, I shall with divine showers
in aim to fervently execute the undone deed, correctly,
so that the horrid deeds of the epitaph may be omitted.

Unto Whence

Though I possessed the desire of thousands,
and to put my possessions in a file
along the lines of The Great Wall,
tickle them with the flicker
of a feather pulled from the turkey,
a gift from a Prince of Power and Wealth,
would all turn the whispers of my articles
into a clamour of chaos.

Toil did I to dig each one out,
Day in and day out I slogged!
one after the other,
My human instinct instigated me to 'more'
Nevertheless enjoyed possessing them.
'Placed my articles in a fort so strong,
Supported by a thousand pillars.
Statues of Turquoise to perfumes......
Past carvings of the finest ivory
to splendid Chandeliers.

I laid an array of a pantheon of desire
all that any could ever posses in this world.
Many a men I dealt that possessed my desires
Many never lift the spade, few lifted it though.
I lay amidst the fluttering desires
to guard every bit with all my life.
With guards to watch thieves
and gadgets of sophistication around them......
Until I was shaken by Her through Him
that I really got down to think of a roof for myself

and left all my earthly possessions in the debris
To find more of heavenly grace, love,
Rebirth, inner joy, salvation, et al.
to nearer my God.

Of thousand pillars made of dust turns to dust.
Of metals from the soil back to soil,
Of past return to past,
I to where I belong,
To the soil and to the sea...........
To whom I am possessed
Not on the face of the Earth.

Wet clay

The scene is set, the stage is set
Spick and span curtains.
The nervousness of the crew rumbles,
They put their best not to tumble.
Briskly walking is the director
putting up his last touches,
For he believes he must have the last say.
The cast all brightly costumed,
Murmuring and memorizing lines
Which only the lips showed.
Excited audience gathered by
multiplications count.
Usherers putting up a smile
for that is what their orders say.
Out-comes the master compere
Tumbling over his word.
Whatever! the show must go on.
Dancers in costumes,
shaking bums, twirling hands
smooth moves, beautiful curves
moving hip and clapping hands;
The magical spell of the dancers.
To what an audience wanted more
There was no more, the evening had to move on.
Then, elaborately and articulately throwing
On dialogues, the actor makes moves.
Look at the hall actor, no body.
Recollection to present tense,
I realized what a tumbled thought
Of a youth is.
Think twice, strange happenings
Of a tumbled mind, strange thoughts!
So strange, yet perpetuating a poem out of it!

Courage in faith.

Stood the vanguard with valour
Against the marching thousand.
Set to hold the fort gallantly
Sail to a triumphant victory,
Gripped with toes affirmed to the ground.
The cheering mass a conviction,
Of eager courage, burnt their eyes.
When all at once, a timidity
To see the rival roar,
And flee from him that soar and
At the enormousity of his size
Then, send many squeaky pretenders
And align the crooked charlatans, exposed.
Verily, a sight not foresighted.
Verily, a pandemonium of utter shock
Hail, then, the son of soil,
Springing from the cowardly soldiers,
Who took the chance to challenge
The giant to a bout.
Little did on lookers know
That the faith he has in him
Held The Almighty,
And humbly steps a step forward,
To vanquish his rival
When he flings a sling
The pebble that hit the giant
Possessed a greater faith than the giant himself.
Hurrah, to see the rival retreat.
Defeat was as close as the hilariousity
The giant had, in seeing the weakling come.
Then, the hysteria drowns into enlightenment.
Of victory cries, it was in the heart.

In Conscientiousness

Shielded in a hardness of a walnut
Is his conscience, for even if things sell
at the price of nature, he is not swayed
amidst all temptations on his way.
Lie he may under oppression,
None may move his state to depression.
The bundle of strength keeps him on within.
Never shall he hold his head higher than it ought to be
Nor below than all he is.
Ever, does he not argue for what
but to keep himself, bargains for all his dues.
Strong at heart but not hard,
Nevertheless, believes in hardships
for life without battles is to eat fruitless fruit.
Temptatious devils of his encounter,
many a times show golden highways.
But, yes, he confides in his conscience
for his will to carry on, goes on increasing
for the man who pursue greater heights
In a nutshell, is a man whom men will say man.

The Solitary Tree

The solitary tree,
Amidst the solitude of a rocky hill.
Stretching itself,
Proud as it can be
Feeling freedom to the full
cause it knows
the service to human it give
Can never be paid back.
Yet, alas! it knows
Its days are numbered
for its last service to human
- *ITS DEATH*

It Was 'Time'

T'was that,
kept me thinking
T'was that,
systematized the world
T'was that,
determined one was late........
rarely early!
T'was time,
I get swept by.

O time, O time
How hard you throw
your hard realities.
A moment passed
you throw love in the air.
A moment text
you throw hatred everywhere
A friend I must say- in it
you even rule our in-betweens

O time, O time
How hard you throw
your harsh realities
It it 'I' that is
hardest hit,
but then, when the time is right
the falcon strikes!
And I strive........
to survive.
O time, O time

A Secret Wish

Listen to my heart
It moans in thirst
It longs for freedom
Let it have the divinity,
my heart seeks it.

Listen to my heart
A friend, I say
Indeed a friend he was.
A friendship it longs.........
my heart seeks it.

Listen to my heart
Has it been hurt
Has it been torn
Did I make a mistake......an answer
my heart seeks it.

Listen to my heart
A solace in him I find
In him I confide
A divine friendship
my heart seeks it.

14th August 'more than 50 years after Independence.

Hark, the joyous sound
of celebrations and festivity.
The loud drums and cymbals
that dance beautifully to mine ears
but, what pain, the pain
that beats an unsubstantiated boast.
    Jolly O me, to find a passer by,
    that tells me of a remembrance,
    that which is celebrated year upon year
    when all at once, join a voice
    proclaiming newer heights.
Through the streets and paths of the city
thundering sparks of 'nationalism',
where I unnoticed lay on four,
expecting a least paise that might fall
out from all the gaudy show.
    Redundant is my presence,
    that a soul feels not to me
    that is ever flickered by feets,
    to where I sense the dimensions
    of the best and thus hardest footwears.
The pompous show goes on
at a cost that I may be left more thirsty,
punishing me with an urge of greed,
that ever chains me all ways.
Must I be but bounded on
such a day or either of pomp,
when a nation calls in celebration
of its commemoration of an Independence Day?

Harmony

In the shimmering twilight of a new day
rises a life revived,
To the tune of flutes that float
and fly like sparkling facets
Calls on to the people of the Pineland
to admire the rising pink pinion of the fowl
that flutters in full form.
The shrill songs of tones from the Oak's
enhances the extravaganza of the orchestra.
    More to it, the sparkling sweet of sun rays
    do glitter the gleaming green of grasses,
    where a rabbit hops in steps to escort
    a long awaited event in readiness to rejig
    as in a fay that marks good beginning.
    Flavouring to a fantasy favour,
    does fragrance of flowers add up.
To yet, of what a reality is wonderland
do not we realize we live in it, perhaps,
as holocausts of magnificence
When all we have to do is admire it.

Imagination

The unattached size and length,
of an unending wind,
doth to every stretch there is room to more
in more and more it goes
through unending circle of a maze.
Of a stage to where we are
and to progress in our ways,
a progress by slow stretches!
To think, little a century past
was beyond thought
that we may explore it new worlds,
But then a long way we now are past
to reach more than just explore new worlds.
For all have it, yet to benefit a few
who stretches his imagination
thus positively change things,
Still he stretches it,
to make the Impossible - possible

A vagabond's delight

Single out in yet a crowded world,
Companions none he has,
not one for him
amidst the bubbles of people
Wanderer, yet he lives
to live the next day.
Search he for nothing by one
yet to what he seeks
he does get it.
To the beauty for wandering
he is happy for there is none
neither to scold him ruthlessly,
for he is guest everywhere he goes.

Nothing to bother such a man,
for fear he not of death,
for fear he of God.
For doth his riches lies in his heart,
Therefore in being a solitary wanderer
he believes he has all reasons to be always happy.

The Other Side

Wandering in a hollow cave,
dark and deep,
sends a shiver to mine nerves
the way is dangerous and hard to keep
still every step in fear
the heart begins to sink,
the desertedness, of peer
who always were none but athletes
upon the goods of times
show their backs upon times of trial
and feel a Judas Kiss piercing
to release repid tears
that ever more weep with betrayal
and upon the indignation meted out
by false amities upon me.

Rejoice, to a voice within
that leadeth a guiding factor
to a happier side
free from malicious baits
in no more living upon a rack,
and find a hand to reach
and stand by, until the stars are reached.
For the world has many
in steadfastness to help
only if a brighter light
is not out done by darkness,
to begin find a happier side of life
within oneself.

The Sun May Rise Again

Such was a time once,
Where mountains and rivers flowed
towards the plentiful destination,
Synchronised to flow unopposed.
The land I long to see,
Shall no more bear a charm
that charmed me spell bound
and think it no less than a dream
giving me much ado to realize
where a dream is or not at all.
At once a thousand Pagodas,
beautifully scattered,
all that posses the glory of days past
and reflect the splendid spires.
Back and forth, I glanced
to see an endless field
past the lands and past Irrawady,
ever harvesting, abundantly.
From Rangoon to Mandalay
I dream to rough an odyssey.

Halt me, dear friends
lest I give weight to a dream
and mislead me to a weeded garden.
Remind me of what is
that such a land is was.
And now to face the tyranny
of a merciless brigand,
that hails the gun
for it spreads a rapid shower

of fear and misery to rule.
The temple is now a sham,
a business place of evil.
Where beautiful Poppies
form a ravishing golden triangle,
is but an infamous monopoly,
that accentuates superficiality.
Little have I have I read and heard,
in balance to all,
The goods must not be outdone by bad.
However, such beauties couldn't but
be true, if not ditto.
How I long to see, a land
devoid of the maladies it bear,
so that a little light may shine
to undo a whale of darkness,
if it is to be so
I shall extol a kingdom in exuberance.

Rusty Barriers

The sad misery of many hearts
that suppress voices
upon being burdened yet
by the heavy rules of myths.
That such a story goes
that does not honour rectitude
is providing barrier to strife
and scrape off what is deserved and earned.
That who is born of the same labour
under similar biological process
and equal heavenly blessings
is shredded to be captive
in petty engagements which ranks subordinate
to his gifted gifts of life' propeller.
That who is born no less a talent
or a suppressed ability and capability
is set to set on where his weaker
perception and ejection level lies
is ever left to suffer,
while humanity becomes a bigger sufferer
of suppressed resource.
All to attribute to the
larger than life myth of 'caste'
to live in scorn and spit.
Of a wastrel who prefix high sir
and live the tyranny of authority
that subdues the right
to make it wrong to their willy purpose.

Hath not the sun set on nobility
that casts rigid lines.
But thunders had proclaimed
that every man was born equal
not to be subjected to lives

not to be subjected to lives
leave alone servitude.
Nullify and throw new slogans
that ever horrendously demand
and equal platform for equals,
for the prince was once a pauper
and the pauper was once a priest
where ever the roots lie,
be it the Garden of Eden
or the African wild lands,
none was bestowed with nobility,
none with power or pelf,
but so true is that after all is said and done
there is more through the lanes
where mercilessly flogged
is a mind that suffers injustice
while another believe that who is of a lower class
is to be flogged.
Of fate shrivelled into the well
tied into the world with disgrace
is lived upon the rack.
There stands life upon a million racks.

My Friend : A Science Student

O'Jove! the fate of the child,
who yearns for time and time
for, but to read his science.
The burden upon him lay
so heavy a stress, he walks bent.
When all his waking hours
do pass by reading science,
Poor thing, his eyeballs bulges as if the strain will
render him to a state of swells.
It seems to pass that the head he hold
has do swelled and hence bulged to disproportion.
For the food and drinks he take
his taste is that of chemicals and acids
for all what is there his mind is it.
And when he do his works,
quick he is to reduce his load
by laws of physics.

To the *unbalanced* child
the world seems a thing
that even at times, wear his socks,
and put it the other way round
although his intentions were not it.
The child who reads science
is a *creature* yet to be a worth.
Again, the *insane* boy
is neither happy nor sad
but slogs to live the day
with half an open eye
still nothing will stop him from reading his science.

To Eternity

The intimate closeness,
the loving care,
the open air-
that is shared by a brother
with a sisterly love is truth.
The admiration of each other,
strong coaliations
that bonds a brother
with a sisterly grace is truth.
Where apt from off a same womb
is siblings evolved to love
is how an earth was to function
in revolving to spin ages.
Where there a brother guards a sister,
a brother a brother, a sister a sister
what end may whatever the beginning have
is life based upon so godly a bond
that such a bond is only second to one
and in sharing so a bond with divinity
upon the heart of the receiver
and the giver, is God itself
and so rejoin to being second to none.
With times now a newer face,
is such establishment a reciprocal
in killing each other
has selfish deeds held the upper hand
where no more is a brother a brother
a sister a sister.
Life once full of sharing
is life lived upon a uninhibited land
to grab the freshest fruit.
Call on, spirits of righteousness
to bestow that what was,
For heaven, share with a brotherly love,
sisterly love..........
To eternity, to eternity..........

Buddy

My Buddy was the greatest.
Never could we think of a day,
would we not even dare to think,
a day when he and I must part ways;
Must that day happen?

Pleasant exchange of greetings
within ourselves silently in progress
Least spoken of and never speaking of me
is my Buddy .
I declare my little wealth to him
and in humble acceptance he shared it,
Most concentrated is that little wealth
that it does not become diluted.

To Buddy I called out
apt is his reply, be it the oddest hour
of day or night,
Thunder or lightning
I proclaim my Buddy is the greatest.
Buddy stays in a room
in my heart now, his demands
are not much and if so
I don't fail him.

Time concludes and so
Buddy goes but his marks won't
that we thought of so wonderful a plan
to remain so close-
We exchanged our shadows
and so as we depart I bear
his shadow and he mine.
My Buddy was the greatest.

Beyond Every Horizon

A blossoming life blooms
as in course of divine touches,
It still wanders in ways of clay,
leaning to and forth it is moulded.

Shattering roadblocks through the way,
Unthought unfortunates, hard lies
heavy battles and worst of worsts.
Still, to this is the armour
of human thought of the ability to dream
beyond horizon's far bound.
Dreaming inspirational encouragement,
the beauty of surpassing limits.

All shall never be lost,
be it a caravan of carcasses.
A ray of hope to he who dreams,
A bright new life to drowning people.

To every nightmare, dream on
to find a rainbow
sparkle beyond the turbid
cloud of life.

Gold-Plated Claws

Thou strikest with magnificence,
Gold plated dreams,
Undreamable pleasure, your tools are.
For once you strike, you are aggressive
you stop not, never!
    To blinding millions you leadeth
    easy wide roads,
    To blinding millions you make
    easy good codes.
Showing Castles, you entrap.
Within moments you entangle
your prey into never ending webs.
To the first time you enter the blind
Nice he wonders, in yearn for more
Twice he connects you, more he yearns.
To now a third he live in a world
of untold lies and falsity.

Shout I then, for you hit the vulnerable
tenderly coaxing them.
For so many a damage you committed
many a torn families to communities
to nations to society.
Fear me then, to sue you
for I shall wake humanity.

Tragedy

Of the motherly love, tenderness,
the boy received, he was well.
Filled with showers of parental care,
the boy was happy,
Happy enough to forget hell.
The soft touches he received,
like other mothers', his was full of aspirations.

Fulfilling her duty to see a ward
fulfill the very ambition of his
through ways of destiny,
she slogs for his sake.

To leave no ironical stone unturned,
the boy stabs his mother
in a most tormenting way.
To an objective of selfishness
rather than to wait,
for what was already his,
the ungrateful child wanted his!
Too late was it that more than love
a lesson of morals was not implanted
death deep,
To a boy whose unkind deed
will never be forgotten and forgiven.

Punctuation

I looked around ....nothing new
Ahead lay the black rock,
Behind - the pine trees.
Dark clouds blocked the Sun,
Cold breeze froze me to death.
Then, at last as the warning foretold
Fell big drop of rain......
Taking shelter beneath the black rock,
I let time pass by waiting for the rest
By noon, creeping out of the clouds
was the rainbow........

I looked around—— a clear sight
My foot firmly rooted to the ground
In steadfastness to continue.

Beginning of the Beginning

When hatred sparks fire,
Heat of untamed magnitude furies
Across lands of innocence
A raging torment storms
and sweetness to bitterness
Unsaid lies line the surface,
Compelling tales of accusations
flashes past borders.
The violent gun shots
of life taking steels
do beleaguer the horrid ill will
to a state of saturation but, halt
to a accommodate more anger,
that do in fits of rage grow evermore.
Unaware of how much harm
it causes to every life.
While all this need not
be born into his world.
Talk peace of a heavenly world,
Unattained will it remain
Until a benign touch of love
ceases the sparks that adds fuel
to fire that fights fire.
Until such time is coal heaved
Upon a heart, till love to begin
learns to begin.

Humour out of a 'Bookworm'

A book in his hand is a must
and if it is not, it means a bewilderment
which ought to be investigated upon.
If so he withhold a book by no reason
then the case is rare and yet to happen an occasion.
The dullard does not enjoy a game
nor posses a spirit of team work
which befits his idiology as he
studies only for himself.
To such a point he reads his books
that through dim light and bright
he has changed the feature of his eyes.
He does not enjoy the pleasure of youth,
and burries his creative potential dead
in the same way he dies of stage fright.
Does not even realize the passing time
and so goes on to read books, and
eventually rots his practical imagination
that makes him handicapped to handle life.
Sinful is his idea of the cafeteria,
even worse is to merrymake with friends.
For such a boy lives in the past and
all that he scores are dust to survive.
He eventually dies in the wide ocean of reality,
unable to swim through barriers
of ethics and characters of human life.
Drowns as a looser-
the simply complexed life of the body
and all he is now stands to be lovingly called
- a 'Bookworm'.

An Unsung Hero

In the wilderness of the jungle
between the heat of beasts
where life rises and falls
upon the metre of death.
Near to the beastly rude
He positions himself,
to capture that with his instrument,
Quick he must be.

In the wilderness of waring lands
between the heat of fire and cannons
where life once hit
is left upon the coffin.
Amongst the fighting men
He focuses anything,
to capture that with his instrument
Quick he must be.

Living on the edge
in sake of many unfortunates
to behold themselves
in beastly forms if not a beast itself.
Getting through to men
of their nearness in ettiquette, to a beast.

Alas, further falls victim
to the rage of one another.
Yet, for all his dedication, many a times
a brave soldier of himself is unsung.

Lost to Time

The glitzy ballroom,
Goblets holded with style.
O' the glamour of the night,
The peak of enjoyment was ....
but, only bounded by time.
    A myriad faces, all strangers
    all but one.
    Towards her did I then glance
    to catch a glimpse of her.
    Shinning eyes, I was struck
    only within her eyes could I be freed
    Secrets bursting out.
    To each other we're bound, I'd thought ....
                                        ....forever
'Adieu'; my heart........it was broken
Distant words too softly spoken
Cold depths, cold breaths
Autumn begins to draw
All I see began to frost,
My beautiful friend
I thought I' d be bound by you.........forever.

But to time you have been lost,
It was by time I was bounded.

Then I Rest With Nature

Upon a land I may ask,
My pale brooding body must lie,
Where man is in oneness with wild,
Nature as it is created,
to realise the great manifestation.

Upon it where no more ever
shall see destitude yearn with bowls
Neither with raised frail hands.

Upon it where he must learn
to live in harmony with his next door.

Tears shall not more be the insignia of sorrow
rather a reciprocal of it,
and with that, shall it flow in abundance,
Bed of roses I do not ask,
All I ask for, a land,
filled with spirited hearts
where holiness finds serenity
To Paradise of much more
than just gongs of hollow words,
I shall lay in peace
With Nature, for true virtues are Nature itself.

A Pebble in the Ocean

In the busy hob nob of a city
Through swift life fast lies,
deceives an itinerant
of an infamous island of easy life
to a courteous terrain.
When in a mart, a conspicious wave
thus created, elevate to currupt
a guileless mind,
and after that makes him feel the honk and tonks
Of slender cars that dash by
to harass a wandering eye
that spells him bound
to take a deep breath of soot
In the gruelling lot of hubbub;
and busy bypassers,
marching up and down
with no regard who lives
to share a husky hull slowly sinking
with hues and cries of feeble worth,
each to his own cry his own.
Oft the hurly-burly then tranquilizes
to a minimal hush by a hurtle
of clashes between hollow vessels,
all into the trickery of a monopoly
to release a canard of hypothesis.
All at the foot of skyscrapers
that goes on to fool the itinerant
out of his simplistic buffoonery
to charm him more and more
all while an individuality
has been blown along with many more bubbles.

A Parody of Democracy

The eagerness in their eyes,
The crowd all roughed up
in the grounds of a dilapidated fort,
Otherwise a heritage,
However to listen their leader speak
in the scorching heat beneath the sun.
A Demi God they call him
Image of leadership thew bestow
upon him.
With vigour never to loose the elections,
repeated slogans after the other
in anticipation of their leader
the new face of the party.

A full hour out of time
the leader is on his way
after delivering a tone of boasts
that underline the greatest democracy of the world.
Whatever, the crowd grows
when all of a sudden
emerges a rival party
to massacre each other
pouring out 'patriotic' hearts
vehemently supporting a democracy
but............what!

To uphold a game of politics
but yet killing democracy itself.
How unclear ever is the truth
that in killing a democracy, in misery
is elections held at the cost of its cause
that ever concludes to an unclear,
Vague answer how the unripe fruit
falls aground before it ripes.

The worms that suck vitality in it,
the birds that peck upon the spines............

Bunking to 'Town'

I had once upon a time
from bounds that I was clutched
with a buddy and his;
ran out of what my liberty grants.
    Through Knolswood, through dark woods.
    I climbed to reach The Mall,
    exasperated and half drawn was 'Sudden Death'
    The sweet pleasure of disobedience!
I purposed not an official visit
but for to calm a growling belly
at the most, I should sip an aerated water
had the dermatologist not threatened me.
    For the time was fast,
    the pleasure of self imposed freedom,
    when I do what I was forbidden
    that way, that all beings are!
The height of excitement and ecstasy
came poping up the lift,
and flight was not for me,
the Master knew not what to say.
    Past the chilly night,
    I melted with fear,
    Of which the same the Master's purpose was,
    I dreamt of canes, and pipes and sticks.
The early rays of sun
that shook me up,
did voice the Master's forgiveness......
But I did not repent.

You Will Be

Yell ye youthful young,
In yearn for flight
along the bounds of your rights
that when you are shouted upon
cry not, disturbed.

Yowl not, youthful young,
for your days to wither
your cocoon is near and sure.
Keep strong to quarrels,
to strike hard at right moments.

Yelp at him, ferociously
to he who unduly wrong you.
Save yourself to courage,
Be not moved by common
for you will soon master yourself
and all you deal, in being a master of yourself
to strive to be good citizen in adulthood.

From Innocence..........

Thunderbolts strike across skies
and dark warning clouds splat the sky.
Then, spits sparks in darts
to beautifully seen with eyes as work of art.
There lies the beauty of downpour
where many of us do join in choir,
In the coolness of the monsoon.
Shower just puts me to delight,
Reviving me to renew in life,
In mirth and laughter do I resolve
in the ambience of kiddish cheers,
that though the dismay of the matron
I even geared up to face a hullabaloo.
In I went even as I ran through Patios
to smell sweet Earth that lets showers
percolate to depths to cool it.
Do at these times with peers
speak of bygone in vividness
and do try to cover enjoyment
in likes of childish habits,
Where above all, lies a fact
that everyone enjoys childish adolescence
but to think of events to come
do temptations feelings subside
All do apprehend the joy of rains
but marks the margin is a clog of mind
which says certain bounds in 'respect' behaviour.

The Second Last Chapter of Volume-I

Time flows by,
at gasps of thoughts,
fast as the illusions
that the magician misses
out of his clutches,
Which moves ahead as he raises his hand.
A step ahead, never behind.

Through the wheel have I also spun
having a circle of sun left for the leave.
When I was a child that shuddered
at thoughts of angry matrons,
I bare could comprehend leaving school,
I could not comprehend the feeling
I only saw my seniors in nostalgia.

Half a decade, to sound it long, past
am I now in the room nearest to the exit,
and sad to see a senior still the same.
I know I too must face a bitter winter,
of struggle to come to terms of beginning anew
and ending to begin, the other side
of public tests and parents' scare.

I had once been put on the verge
when I parted a home where heart was
to dwell where the mind is searching the heart.
Living in a sub consciousness of time,
All I hold, the memory of parting dears.
To see myself more like a cat,
it loves the home the master next,
to define a coil of nostalgia,
of parting and beginning,
of ending and waiting,
Then till the time I hold the knob
I shall continue ....tomorrow
and tomorrow will come soon.

With a Living Past

Sweet thoughts that generate from the past,
is a magic of memory.
The machine that never was invented
is instilled in us by every passing moment,
The quality of which depends widely
from how a time at hand is spent
to how good a recollection is made.
The essence of reality it posses
that is ever undoubted
is a truth burried deep in the past.
An entertainment with truth
had never been an imagination yet,
not surpassed by any other entertainer.
Never from generation down generation
proving better than before,
ever rolling the reels of fantasy
one after the other leadeth
an audience to a wonderland,
sad, the show opens only for one,
at a time, infinite times!
The wonderland brings back the dead
that evermore play as in life
To wonder, such a machine
never has been discovered.
In spending time aloof
and devoid of distractions,
in a deep thought, with a smile
casts and binds a spell
that accelerates the ride
to an immortal past, stored in the crystal ball
which as matter neither heard nor seen.
Feel it to realize a magic box,
within oneself is a living memory.

A Call to Unite

Through the array of villages,
past the rural lane,
the heavier part of the same
country where oft through ages
have not seen the same
but believed in petty gauges
of ignorant forefathers.
Till the dark thatches
in learning a blind logic
with teachings that never hatch
unable to bring forth magic.
But now in constant awakening light
a rural mind learns to read and write
to add fuel to a train to heights.
When the nurturing voice is moulded
to enlighten his task of dough
to sharpen many more still clouded,
to fulfil a long wish to read rough
the missing words of his deeds loudly.
That once he may read the statute of the land
in teaching others he lends a helping hand.
Then, through small progress,
sowing seeds of awakening
there is no turning back, nor long for recess.
The thunder of wonder will propel
the mass to spell a name, read a name,
edit a name, write a name.
One voice one call, One name one country
One spirit one India.

Twist and Sham

Complications of an attachment
that vividly highlight a bond,
that engages themselves to promises
and seek out through starry nights
for a rendezvous warm to keep
a chilling frosty night at bay,
to breathe an unchained melody.

And in a matter of time cuddle
to hold the spasms of excitement
when through the isle the bride
is led to tie a knot to make
what was two into one
and both the bride and groom
swears with all their hearts,
to form an association of love
and hold the frame of a family,
never to let a chapter of it
go to the deep desert of throng.

Little over a year since the day
has little symbols of sync
like puppies gone down the list
of compulsory rites
performed each morn
and the signet ring now rugged
the cert, dust and blotted,
genuine words spelt out
in the forefront of the ornate church
vaguely trebble in sight and mind.

It is not a hurricane that bifurcate
the world of living cubs
to bear an utterly shammed home
to wonder in a home
where the virtues of the likes of love
are not comprehended,
is a tale of fairies that once were
and instills-' a promise must be broken',
to the outlines of life,
shall then bear a vengeful head
that shall loose morality
into repeating history,
is times now changed to how
insignificant is a marriage rendered to.
If history were to repeat itself
then why so not the strength of marriage
or was it never how we picture it.

Insult in pity

A city of joy that once,
lies doth dotted of leapers,
vagabonds that frown
and sadly a picturesque of sorrow.
Where oft the Lala walks
in pity of a thousand hands;
drops in a coin that's worth
Pitieous is his heart to see
a child that scoops the dirt
out of thirst from a broken line.
Feels he pity then equally
to the ageing lady that murmer blessings
and urge himself to drop another coin.
Even in a soft heart,
he encounters a limping bond
that pleads his case
Lala walks on ignoring
however with a pity growing within.
Pleads the bond with strong words
in humbleness bends to his feet,
Lalaji is not convinced to burst.
Slowly in softening his heart
the bond that touch him
annoys him to make the miser
a generous man to fling out
two coins for him.
Urgrateful of more than what he deserves
a scornful bond abuses
While Lalaji moves on with ever
a piteous heart, insulted.

Retribution

Sad tales of sorrow,
ripping apart all that on way.
Sorrow eyes crying of
that vandalises with no bound.
Furious deeds of the unknown,
Crevices the hold beneath the feet,
lengthening it to a crooked line
miles and miles from whence,
To engulf the hard built poise
but yet deep now.
That do dwell in another,
gushed upon by a stampede of strength,
deeply thrusted like a seed,
embedding dwellers to cope
when all the breath to them is rested.
Drawn along the thickness of downpour
that evermore dirts the highway than bathe,
vulnerable to drink in the swift rapids.
Whirling in public to unroot
elements of deeply rooted bottom.
Growing in strength and volatile.
Passes by life and death in moments.
After the halt of it the
Shrick cry of a broken limbed gives relief,
While with ever grim eyes the rest look across
the barren land of darkness.
Such robust manifestation is whence
men has discrimilately plundered,
is still to be thought when
a resistence to such a revenge nurture,
in doing so we pay lesser a penalty
accounting the rest to our sins.

This Loneliness

A multitude at a glance
wonder why this feels
a loneliness of self.
Hard to live, Hard to fight
Briskly pacing up the hill
and down the hill of thoughts.
Caging the innocent,
What hard a confinement
that jitters self urge,
so hard the pull is to render
such to madness.
Harsh walls of such made confinement
Chains to an unknown bar.
In vividness to jump the heart pounds
all to enjoy the bunch,
Such closeness of a lonely mind
that do moan and groan
to solitude that is evermore
occupied with life,
in neither nor loneliness.
Peace be of the bang noise
that rattles to sleep as a lullaby.
Such state we travel
thus that such peace
means such to create choas
that now dispel loneliness
amidst the 'disorder' is a peace.

Out of the Mahal

O white, Pure white.
Hallowed queen of monumental spires,
of specless virtuosity,
that radiance a glorious beauty
and even under the shadow of the clouds
is a wonder that stands out.
Enthralled, with speechless words
I mumble in awesome wonder,
Carried by an enchanting sight.

Deep the ravines of thought
is bolted a provocation,
what love, pure love
so great a man that built thee.
For she, the fair lady deep in sleep,
that once a love was love forever
but now entombed in death
and see how awfully dispised is vanity,
and is that do astonished flock for,

While the majestic waters of Yamuna flow
into evenance, still sparkles
life to the living insignia memory,
the world is bereft of speech
to chart an euphony
either of the splendour of the structure
or the love that propelled it.
Into never ending arena of doubt
is he entranced to, who goes
to search the light which lit the hearts
while all in gasp, is led to depth
at all is yet a Chapter of death.

Please Smile

A message that sparkles clearly,
outdoing a crystal piece!
is an expression
That symbols a million words,
and enhance a beautiful world.
The ever unspoken message
do smite a rivals evil
in tranquilizing loops at level.
Gentle errands of love
spreads a purpose like wild fire
in the faces of myriad.
The delight in receiving
to such that perceive
is ought to be returned
lest a receiver is inhuman.
Nothing is as powerful
to stand trial against
an agent that penetrate deep
to the deepest bottom of a heart,
In pursuence of a breath taking world
Put on easy smile, always.

Tears of Fear

Curse the hands that rapped the child,
doom it to misanthropy
of killing gentle humane,
that amounts for tears that burst
and flow down the checks
of the lively lass,
young and pretty, the ponytail
She hath upon the back
of crimson red and the bow
that wounds her collar
portrays a treasure house
of the joy in seeing a pleasant being
but now, has cracks on lines
where terrible drops of tears flow
presenting a sober show
that outcast a blooming flower.
While all the fault she hath committed
is the sad phenomenon of forgetting.
The fragnant harkly she held
tight in the fist with anger,
with all the liberty she had,
to cry and weep and feel.
When time took its course
a phenomenon had yet again happened,
in fear of the fury of the bellows
and blow of the lady,
A girl had succumed to fear
and excuses herself of aching Stomach
and ails herself to swallow Pills,
although a frightened child is not ill.

Behold the Reflection

The enchanting eyes of a maid
The sharp reflections it bears
The thinline that outlines it
The well positioned nose,
The smooth curves carved on
The gentle softness it holds.
The rose red lips of' hers,
The perfect thickness and
The even more sparkling words it shoots
Embedded in a rightly fitting face.

What perfection of features
do hold to be called a beauty ;
Not true, though holds high of said
that beauty lies in the eye of the beholder,
and so in following, a beautiful
face is framed into perfection.
Hold so beauty to a beholder
Then so beauty lies
much beyond the surface.

To prove well beauty is
proclaimed in the depth of truth
That is universally beautiful.
To that who carries a picturesque
Doth carry hollow depth that
do camouflage the intrinsic beauty.
Which may lie much deeper,
Nevertheless, is reflected on the appearance.

Justice for my Mother

Sing to me with tenderness,
Cradle me to sleep
and lay your arms upon my sleep
it purposes softer than pillows.
While to every tear I shed
Mother, don't cry.
Loving ever more and more
you are indispensable to me.

The caring touches of your's
through tumult of sickness
which do provide more healings
than all edible pills,
The cure to all my pains
lies deep in the depths of your heart
which spurts in form of love.

Of the violent storms,
that do pamper me,
You are a pillar of support,
ever near, ever close.
Never with a dimmer hope
in you, never with a lesser strength,
when I do reach out,
I do find the grip to more than hope.
Forgive me if I cry to hurt you
for I cannot bear to hear men weigh
of thy love with worldly worth.

A Prayer of Awakening

To sing a song with the air,
to live amidst a forgotten land,
to freeze the face with cool breeze,
and the pleasant rustle of leaves,
leaves one forth a deviated norm
to a trance of dumb ecstasy.

Upon being shook up by an event
of great reconciliation
is a jerk shot upon the mark,
but down a bottom line
jovially push a task
to myself in future,
for I believed in a belief
of mine, to that a work later
done, is better done.

In unending cycles of proscrastinations
lies a burden enormous
until a net answer evolves
of the zero totality of a work done.
From such a circle of fooling oneself
Our Father in Heaven, save us
from habits that harm
more so from those that doom us.

Acceptance

True to his labour in good terms
is to extract the sweet of his toil
that seeps out a surface to flow below.
The sweat of toil proves manure
to riches of all dimensions.
For every time the spade is lifted
showers of good fortune befall.
The smiling motivator behind
depths of heart, for he who toils
brings forth the truth of living,
in a hardship for survival.

In the working flesh is a
living soul filled with spirit
of joy in realizing
simple ways of life,
Of a rewarding deed done
in so reaping heaps
to a toiling flesh is
always hopeful of divine blessings.
For he who yearns
he may get it only if he
toil hard to strike at it.

Duties and Friendship

Well known it is-
At the marriage of two forces
erupts a bond, energy must it be called.
No different is the way of friendship.
Oft and oft I wonder,
Where this very bond draw it magic.
Wonder I would, till I harp to sickness.
Pure as it is, floweth to eternity,
please do not stop or cease it
for it carries along-fraternity.
Think once, think twice
Isn't it divine.
Think over it, again and again.
Indeed ' its divine.

Passing within our amidst
all the time-unnoticed.
This is friendship.
Risen above petty things and all troubles
give what may for it.
Die, if you must for it.
For unto earth was man born
To fulfil a task of servitude to one another
Therefore, fulfil a task,
a compulsion of duty on Earth
by friendship; it is best served.

Reasons to Challenge

In mock and ridiculation
your destiny seem to lay
how so by no perchance
is truth levied upon a belief as such.
A wastrel them upon you
them that are dumb,
in doing so, a bigger cause
of being a wastrel they pour upon themselves.

Hush the tears that flow,
When a warlock bechance
them those guilty of mockery
shall be crippled to paralysis.
Let the blind laugh
While you vault on in life
For they comprehend not the wand
that has so graciously been thrusted
by sparks of divinity,
an honour above others.
In trust spite a disheartened show
and challenge yourself,
the words that lessen your fortunes,
for them to behold a miracle.

The hope is true in a resolution
that challenges hope against hope.
Even the mirage can become a reality
when past the desert you fight,
to get a reward well received.
In willingness to challenge
that who look down upon you,
Knowing well the best gifts
bestowed upon by the one above us,
always has a reason.

Dark Clouds

Oblivious of rampant havoc
caused under the black cloth
by intruding forces of gluttony;
is days past the sweet by gone.
Where upon living under wrath
of human instinct of 'More'
is a corrosive agent of disruption
that creeps a peeping society
that ever in unspoken terms express,
hallowed be the nature of concern.

What so ever be a case, of unbelievable purity
is a battered mask underneath
None to object, none to nullify
a wider picture behind which
is the darker truth.
From patriotic deeds to gentle games
Which immemorial of past
has men considered sincere
and genuine, are not to be so.
Has in yester years revealed
a contemporary taboo
of excessive craze and crush.

The bottom line of which rules
a limit not to be exceeded,
a reminder of childhood roots
never to hoard in excess
has proven how never should man
succumb to his urge to go beyond a limit
However, above all pure plays,
sincere games and true emotions
that adhere to the face of the Earth and beyond
is a relevation to only lone the almighty,
creator of heaven and earth in excess
more and more.

The Circle of Recoilation

To the happy village
Where the sun never set
To many smiling faces
Which never frown
The sweet delight of illitracy,
charms the simplicity of simpletons.
The virgin land they sleep upon,
Where one find day came foreigners
with a 'Ball'!
teaching them a new game.
Let wait, let patience
for first the whole village
sets to work upon their
hill to make it flat.
Happily, now they learn new sport
Strangely for the new sport
doth teach the rude-gentleness
with undoubted spirit
the village put its mind and boby
in full support of the sport.
To what a sleepy yet happy village
a sport has made it burst,
with life as a part of life.
One day, with force
and strength they kicked the ball
and down it went, down to where the ball
is lost forever.
Heartless hollow smile returns
yet again to the village.